Forgiveness

Published by Rodney Hogue

Copyright © 2008 by Rodney Hogue, all rights reserved.

First printing 1997
Last revision 2008
Edited 2017

ISBN 978-164007440-8

No part of this book may be reproduced, stored, or transmitted in any form or by any means, electronic or mechanical, including photocopying and recording, or by any information storage or retrieval system, except as may be expressly permitted in writing by the author/publisher.

Rodney Hogue Ministries
Abilene, Texas

All scripture is New American Standard Version unless otherwise stated. Used by permission, © 1960, 1962, 1963, 1971, 1972, 1973, 1975, 1977, 1995 by Lockman Foundation, all rights reserved.

Scripture quotations marked (NIV) are taken from the HOLY BIBLE, NEW INTERNATIONAL VERSION ® Copyright © 1973, 1978, 1984, by International Bible Society. Used by permission of Zondervan Publishing House.

Scripture quotations marked (NCV) are taken from the New Century Version, WORD Incorporated, © 1991, all rights reserved

Printed in US by Instantpublisher.com

Table of Contents

"To Forgive or Not to Forgive" 5

Exactly what is forgiveness? 9

Forgiveness, Reconciliation, and Boundaries.... 15

The Bottom Line:
What does forgiveness do for you?............... 21

What if I don't want to forgive? 25

How bitterness gets embedded
in a heart 33

Tearing down the stronghold of bitterness 43

Rebuilding the area with a godly
stronghold of compassion................... 53

How about those lingering feelings of
unforgiveness? 67

Forgiving myself and forgiving God 71

The Final Word... 76

Introduction

I didn't start out to write a book on forgiveness. As the pastor of my church, I just wanted to help our church members walk in freedom. One day it dawned on me that I spent a huge amount of my time counseling members of my congregation through issues related to forgiveness. The need to forgive and release an offender remains the most common condition I find myself having to work people through. I began to figure out that a majority of the people wouldn't have to come in for a counseling appointment if they could understand and apply genuine forgiveness.

I began to look for resources that efficiently addressed this topic. I looked for something that was easy to read, gave an adequate perspective on forgiveness, easily walked them through the process, and equip them to sustain a heart that continues to forgive. I knew that was a tall order but there are a lot books on the market on the topic of forgiveness. However, most books were so detailed that most of the individuals I was working with would not have had the patience to wade through the exhaustive material and pull out what was good for them and discard what wasn't.

In the early 1990's I began to train our members in prayer counseling which equipped our members to minister to the wounded heart, physical healing, and deliverance. I felt compelled to provide them with a tool to help them in ministering forgiveness. This is when I decided to kill two birds with one stone and put together a very simple tool. That tool became a small pamphlet that was used extensively by those in our church as well as many outside of it. The pamphlet was good not only as a tool for our members to minister to others but would also help those who needed to work through forgiveness issues. Either before or during a counseling session, I would just hand many the pamphlet and ask them to work it through before we met again. Our church office would just print up a bunch of pamphlets and stick them out in the church foyer. The pamphlet would later turn into a workbook, then a brief manual, and finally the book you have now.

I put this book together in order to give a tool that will help facilitate the healing and restoration of the soul, which has been bound by either an unwillingness to forgive or by feeling powerless to forgive. I have tried to keep it as brief as I could so you don't get bogged down, but at the same time be thorough enough to facilitate working someone through the forgiveness process. Reconciliation is a significant issue but I am only going to briefly touch on the reconciliation process. I know there is much more that could be said on that topic, but that isn't my primary purpose.

I also know that the act of forgiveness can be and should be a simple act of the will. However, many really do need to wrestle through this process in order to solidify it in their lives. It isn't uncommon for me to find people who, after making a choice of their will to forgive, still find themselves wondering if they really did forgive since feelings of unforgiveness still linger. Others haven't done the necessary follow-up work to rebuild their heart so that bitterness has no place to return.

It is my hope that we all take the risk of releasing our offenders and learn to live in freedom that is our inheritance in Christ. I pray that as you read this book, you will see the necessity of forgiveness and release every offender you may have in your life. To accomplish that objective, I want you to, first, understand what forgiveness really means. There are too many misconceptions of what forgiveness really is and it requires clarification. I believe that if you really understand what you are doing when you forgive another, you might not be reluctant to forgive, or even struggle with the idea of it. Next, I want to examine how we open the door to bitterness and give it a home in our hearts. The reason we cover this subject is to help unravel the areas where we have entangled ourselves that have kept this door open. In conclusion, I hope to give you some help in creating a heart where bitterness has a difficult time penetrating into it. Wouldn't it be great to walk through life with a Teflon© nonstick spiritual armor, where offenses slide off rather than stick as they are thrown at you daily? Building a heart that quickly resolves offenses is actually the most important aspect of this booklet. It is imperative that our hearts be ruled by a stronghold of compassion so we will react and see everyone – even our offenders – through the eyes of Jesus.

And forgive us our debts, as we also have forgiven our debtors......For if you forgive men for their transgressions, your heavenly Father will also forgive you. But if you do not forgive men, then your Father will not forgive your transgressions.
(Matthew 6:12, 14, 15)

Then Peter came to Jesus and asked, "Lord, how many times shall I forgive my brother when he sins against me? Up to seven times?" Jesus answered, "I tell you, not seven times, but seventy-seven times. (Matthew 18:21-22 NIV)

And whenever you stand praying, forgive, if you have anything against anyone; so that your Father also who is in heaven may forgive you your transgressions. (Mark 11:25)

Be on your guard! If your brother sins, rebuke him; and if he repents, forgive him. And if he sins against you seven times a day, and returns to you seven times, saying, 'I repent,' forgive him. (Luke 17:3-4)

"If you forgive the sins of any, their sins have been forgiven them; if you retain the sins of any, they have been retained."
(John 20:23)

Chapter 1

"To Forgive or Not to Forgive"

"I can't forgive them! You don't know what they've done to me!"

Does that sound familiar? Have you ever heard someone say that? Is that something that you've said? One of the most difficult things God calls us to do is to forgive someone, especially if we have been unjustly wronged by them. Yet deep down inside, for those who have a relationship with God through Jesus Christ, we know that it is the right thing to do.

One can think of all kinds of reasons why you shouldn't forgive someone who had wronged you. You might feel that forgiving is just letting your offenders off the hook. You may feel like they still need to be punished for what that did and your unforgiveness somehow does that. You might be waiting for them to feel remorse and apologize to you and then you might consider forgiving them. You might be thinking that they don't even deserve to be forgiven. Regardless of all the reasons why you might not want to forgive, the bottom line is that forgiveness is the best way to bring you into freedom.

The devil blinds us with the lie: *I am punishing my offender by not forgiving them.* It is as if we think by our refusal to forgive a person we are somehow punishing them. That is a deception. If we think we are getting even with them by refusing to forgive them or that somehow we are hurting them because we will not forgive them, we are embracing this diabolical scheme. The truth is, instead of hurting others, we are actually tormenting ourselves. We become the victims when we refuse to forgive.

Once, a middle-aged man came into my office to discuss the problems in his life. Life was not going so well for this man. As we processed what he was going through, it became evident that he blamed most of his current problems on the childhood emotional abuse he received from his mother. Even as an adult in his forties, he found himself a victim of continual manipulation from his mother. We talked about the call to forgive his mother and release her. At first, he was unwilling. He wanted his mother to experience the same pain by refusing to forgive her, therefore, he continued to harbor resentment and anger. I asked him a few questions like, *"What do you think your mother is doing right now? Do you think she is at home worried and bothered that you have refused to forgive her?"* As he thought about it, he began to acknowledge that she probably wasn't thinking about him at all. She was probably sitting at home watching television, unbothered by his refusal to forgive. The next question I asked him was, *"Where are you?"* He was in my office, processing his anger. In fact, he had spent countless hours in therapy processing his anger against his mother. His job, his relationship with his wife, and his relationship with his children all suffered because of his bitterness. So who was hurting whom? Who was the victim here? Certainly, it wasn't his mother, but himself. He was disabled in life.

The lack of forgiveness produces bitterness and bitterness always puts a person in bondage. When we experience an extremely deep wound, it doesn't seem possible to forgive. We then hold onto our resentment hoping to find some kind of justice for the wrong that was committed. When we live life holding onto prior hurts, we are restraining ourselves from the liberty that was paid for us on the cross. Unforgiveness hinders us from moving forward in life. If we are constantly reminiscing about former offenses and living our lives through our past experiences, those experiences will be the very factors that determine how we see and react to the world. The earlier we realize that forgiveness is the direction to the road of freedom, the faster it will be to walk on that road. We are the beneficiaries when we choose to release those whom we are tempted to harbor resentment against.

We should forgive for the results, but more importantly, we should forgive because it is important to God. God sent His only Son to pay the price for our sins so that there would be no barrier of sin between us and Him. When we look at the great sacrificial price that was made for our forgiveness, it does not take a rocket scientist to figure out how important forgiveness is to God. Jesus gave us the ultimate example as He looked down and saw those who put him on the cross and chose to forgive them. (Luke 23:34) When Christ gives us the command to forgive, He does not give it without already first demonstrating it for us. Compassion dominates! We need to learn to let compassion rule our hearts as we follow after Christ's model.

Even though we know we should forgive, is it really possible to forgive? We can become so overwhelmed with our pain that we do not feel we will ever be able to forgive certain people in our lives. When others talk to us about forgiving and releasing an offender, we may respond with, "I can't." Most often we respond in that way because we are looking at what we can do in our own power.

If you are one who just cannot seem to forgive, let me ask a few questions which might give you another perspective. Have you received the forgiveness that God offers through a relationship with Jesus? Have you personally experienced God's forgiveness of your sins? If you haven't, then there is some credibility to the statement,

"I can't forgive." If you have, then you have canceled your right to hang onto offenses. The day you asked Jesus to come into your life as your Lord, to rule your life, a part of that process involved asking and receiving God's forgiveness for your sins. When you receive God's forgiveness, then forgiving others is your only option. Here's the good news: God supplies the power to forgive. You aren't on your own to do this one! Receiving God's forgiveness empowers us as we live in His grace. Living in His grace means that He gives you the grace to give to others the very things you have received from Him. It is the unmerited inexhaustible power supply that flows from God to us, and through us, to do His will. It isn't an issue of "I can't..," but it is an issue of your willingness to receive the grace from God to forgive as you have been forgiven. Forgiveness is not a natural response to being hurt, but it certainly is a supernatural one that is empowered by our living God. Even though we may feel that we cannot forgive, God supplies us with enough power to forgive.

Chapter 2
Exactly what is forgiveness?

A good starting place is to discover what we are doing when we forgive people or things in our lives. It is important to know what forgiveness is and what it isn't. The devil, the father of lies, uses manipulation to keep us in bondage. Setting the record straight on the truths of "what forgiveness is" may help us release our offender and, at the same time, help us realize the commitments of genuine forgiveness.

Forgiveness first begins with the acknowledgement that an offense has been committed. You cannot forgive unless you admit that someone has offended you. I know this sounds like a no-brainer, but recognizing the situation can be the one grain of rice that tips the scale into the healing process. You can choose to continue to harbor resentment by sweeping it under the rug through denial. On the surface, you may say, "I'm OK. It's not that bad. I can handle it." That may sound and look noble, but it does nothing to bring resolution and healing. You can still stay trapped and eventually accumulate more rubbish by minimizing the effect that another had on your life. On one side, it may be difficult to admit you had been hurt because you think it is unspiritual to admit such a feeling. On the other side, you may not want to admit to carrying an offense because it might reveal a flaw in your character, or you might not want others to think less of you.

One woman was still bitter about her husband's affair and subsequent divorce that happened 30 years earlier. On the outside, she carried the facade of being the perfect Christian woman who had her life together, complete with the spirit-filled Christian lingo. However, from time to time, the bitterness that covered her heart slimed others. Her problem was pride. She had a reputation to uphold. She tried burying her pain, but her pain would not stay buried. To admit she still carried bitterness after thirty years was too shameful and incongruent to her perception of her own spiritual maturity. No doubt, the churches she attended may have contributed to her masks. It was not until she came to a church where it was safe to be sick and not perfect, was she finally able to admit that she was still debilitated.

You cannot restore freedom from something until you will admit it as an area of struggle. The first few steps of forgiveness, in short, begin by admitting you have been offended. You must know that it is not a weakness in your character when another person offends you. You do not need to feel guilty for being simply human. At this point you start with acknowledging the offense. You cannot quickly rid yourself of the offense until you bring it to the surface and call it for what it is.

Acknowledgement of an offense is significant for those who feel they are forced to forget. One woman refused to forgive a family member who had sexually abused her. She thought to do so would mean she would have to live her life in such a way as if the action had never taken place.

Forgiveness doesn't remove or delete offenses from our lives. Forgiveness doesn't mean that you go into denial and forget this ever happened to you. It isn't that you are somehow wiping this event from your life, glossing over the wrongs others did, nor developing a memory lapse of the pain you have suffered. Forgiveness will not erase your memory clean. What forgiveness does is to remove the power of that memory over your life.

Forgiveness doesn't declare that what the offenders did is now OK. You might assume that if you forgive, you are somehow coming to terms with the offense and excusing it. The truth is that forgiveness does not conceal the seriousness of the hurt that the offense may have caused. For example, one man had a business associate take advantage of him in such a way that devastated his business. His belief was that if he were to forgive his business associate for his treacherous actions, it would mean that he would have to diminish the magnitude of the crime. He didn't want to minimize the treachery. His life was a living hell for a season. For him to forgive did not mean that he was no longer affected by the offense. Forgiveness does not mean you have to confess that you are no longer affected by the actions of another or that their actions should not have consequences. Instead, forgiveness takes an offense seriously, without trying to pass it off as an insignificant and trivial matter.

Jesus would describe forgiveness as releasing a debt in Matthew 6:12, *'And forgive us our debts, as we also have forgiven our debtors.* This is a very significant concept if you are to grasp forgiveness. A debt is something owed to us. Every wrong produces an indebtedness that we feel. Have you ever heard someone say, "You owe me an apology!"? If I offended you, then I have created a debt and am obligated to pay it. You will want to make sure that I am penalized appropriately – the punishment fitting the crime. You hope to receive satisfaction as I'm punished for my debt against you. However, for you to forgive me you must release not only my obligation to you but you also must give up any satisfaction you think you would experience whenever I am punished. Forgiveness means that you must release what you are owed and not give your offenders what they deserve. Forgiveness isn't saying that you are not owed something. Forgiveness acknowledges the debt but you are choosing to cancel it. This is the essence of forgiveness – releasing the other person's indebtedness to you.

Let's take it a step further. I just mentioned that Jesus' concept that forgiveness is releasing a debt. To really grasp the idea, let's say that I borrowed a huge sum of money from you. I would, then, have to repay it in order to be released from my debt. What if this debt was so huge that there is no possible way that I could ever repay it? What are your choices if you realized that repayment was never going to happen? What if I borrowed from you a priceless irreplaceable item and then lost it? How could I ever pay back what was so precious to you? You may be holding onto a debt caused by an offence hoping that one day you would collect on it and gain some sort of satisfaction. This is a deception because you will never collect enough to compensate for your loss. The debt is actually worthless since there is nothing the offender can do to adequately recompense you for your loss. As long as you are holding out for that, you are still in bondage to the offender. You need to cut your losses and move on with life.

You might want revenge, but no matter how much the offender may suffer, it still won't remove your pain. The only way to be emotionally free from them is to let go and turn the offender over to Jesus. It is absurd to think that an "I'm sorry" will actually cover your losses fully. It is an illusion to think that somehow the offender's remorse and repentance will eliminate the pain you have been experiencing. It may provide momentary satisfaction, but it does not heal the wound completely. If you think about your relationship with God, telling Him "I'm sorry" enough times will not erase the obligation of your sin. God releases your debt in forgiving you. The only way for you to be free is to release the debt. In releasing the debt you are releasing your tie to the debtor, and the result is freedom! Until then, you are still in bondage to the offense and in bondage to the offender.

Forgiveness means that you are releasing the offender into the care of Jesus who is our just Judge and our Defender. *Never take your own revenge, beloved, but leave room for the wrath of God, for it is written, "Vengeance is Mine, I will repay," says the Lord.* (Romans 12:19)

Have you considered that you might be hindering the justice process because you are attempting to do God's job through your own vengeance? Avenging an injustice is always wrong. When we hang onto an offense, we are attaching ourselves to the offense as well as the offender. As long as we hang on to the offense and refuse to release it, we are deciding that we want to stand in God's place and take our own revenge rather than let our Just Judge do it. In reality, we may be limiting justice because of God's mercy to us. To render justice to the offender it would have to pass through us first since we are standing between God and the offender. It is the mercy of God towards us when the activity of God to render justice is delayed. Having bound ourselves to our offender through retaining the offense and standing in God's role in seeking to render our own revenge, we position ourselves right in the middle of God's line of sight standing between Him and the offender. I can just hear God say at times, *"Will you please just step out of the way and give me a clear shot?"* For God to have access to the offender to bring about justice we must release the offender and the offense into God's hand.

Our reluctance to forgive comes when we feel that forgiveness somehow lets our offender be discharged from what they might have done. Genuine forgiveness recognizes that we do not have the right to become the enforcers of justice. We relinquish that right by committing that person out of our hands and into the hands of God, our perfect and holy Judge. God will deal justly with all. You will not be letting someone off the hook; you will be transferring that person from your "hook" to "Jesus' hook."

Chapter 3

Forgiveness, Reconciliation, and Boundaries

One reason you may not want to forgive is because you fear having to reconcile with the other person. I know some people who are so terrified of having a relationship with someone who has wounded them severely that they actually use their unforgiveness as a wall to create a boundary to stay separated from their offender. However, forgiving a person doesn't mean that reconciliation is the inevitable next step. Reconciliation could be defined as a relationship that is restored. Although forgiveness is the first step in any reconciliation process, to forgive doesn't require reconciling a broken relationship. As God's children, we must respond righteously and take responsibility for our part in any conflict. A restored relationship is not always the primary objective. Therefore, you do not have to become best friends or have a relationship fully salvaged in order to satisfy the conditions of forgiveness. Sometimes reconciliation is impossible because the offender is dead or unreachable. In addition, your offender may not even have any desire to be reconciled.

For example, not having any idea of where his father was, a son believed that he could not forgive his dad. He thought that to forgive meant he had to somehow contact his father and tell him he had forgiven him. He was willing to forgive his father, but felt that somehow his forgiveness didn't really count unless he was able to somehow either verbally or in writing tell his father that he forgave him. Since he didn't even know where to start to find his father, he felt as though he would have to remain in this unsettled state until contact could be made. All he actually needed to do was to choose to release his father's debt against him, which did not require his father's presence.

Another woman thought she couldn't forgive because to do so meant she would have to become friends with the person who had hurt her. The wounding was so deep that she didn't want to be friends. The relationship was really unhealthy. As long as each reacted out their wounded hearts towards each other, it appeared inevitable that they would pile up more offenses against each other with any attempt at reconciliation. Since friendship was out of the question, she did not want to forgive. However, forgiveness isn't optional. She did not realize that in order to release the other person of their sin against her, it did not require her to talk to or confront her offender. She did not have to amend, or even attempt to amend, the relationship in order to forgive.

While forgiveness is always necessary, reconciliation is not. Forgiveness depends on the offended releasing the debt of the offender irregardless of whether the relationship is restored. There are factors that need to be considered. For example, the communication skills and the timing of confrontation required for restoring a relationship may be beyond the capabilities of the parties involved. To try to approach the other person when there is very limited communication skills might leave the relationship in an even greater disaster. Sometimes wisdom recognizes your limitations. I can't tell you the number of times that someone with great intentions of forgiving and reconciling came back to me in worse shape than when they left because their lack of skills got them verbally beat up.

There is also the issue of whether or not your offender is even willing to work through the reconciliation process. Sometimes the offender has no desire to be reconciled at all. You cannot force reconciliation when the other person isn't interested. Then there are times that reconciliation is impossible without some sort of restitution or remorse on the part of the offender. The offended person may need to know how sincere the offender's remorse is towards the situation. In other cases, there may need to be some proof of repentance and change in behavior. These are factors that weigh in for reconciliation to take place but not for forgiveness. Many of these factors are just out of the control of the offended. If all of these issues had to be resolved before you can forgive, then the odds are, it just won't happen. That is why I say that even though forgives is mandatory, reconciliation isn't. Forgiveness focuses on addressing the offense while reconciliation focuses on the relationship and requires both parties to be in agreement to be reconciled, choosing to work through the reconciliation process. This is not in the control of the one who has been offended. Your choice to forgive can never be dependent upon the actions and choices of your offender; it is dependent upon you choosing to release the debt of the offender.

The Bible says to, *"Make every effort to live in peace with all men and to be holy; without holiness no one will see the Lord."* (Hebrews 12:14 NIV) If reconciliation were possible, it would no doubt be beneficial. However, even though reconciliation is preferred, it is not always possible.

If you do decide to make amends, the starting point requires that you admit anything on your part that contributed to the offense. If there is nothing on your part, do not feel obligated to give a "courtesy confession" in hopes of manipulating the offender into a confession of a wrong. When you do make amends, do it in the arena in which the offense is committed. If you were to offend me, but let's say that you did not know that you had offended me, then I don't need to tell you how you offended me. I only need to take it to God and address it with Him. As far as you know, there was no offense, and that keeps it in the arena in which it was committed. The exception is if a person continues to offend people and they are oblivious to their offensive behavior, as a courtesy to them to help them grow, they need to know. Some people are just prone to "drive-by" offenses and are unaware of their behavior and someone needs to help them out. Aside from this circumstance, I generally think it is best not to share offenses if the other person is unaware. It might actually be your "stuff" that caused the offense. Just examine your motivations. My motivation could be that I wanted you to share my pain, and probably to be hurt as well. After all, if I were hurt, my natural response would be for me to share that with you so you feel a little pain as well. To take it to God and deal with it in that arena is my recommended course of action unless God specifically instructs otherwise.

A person once approached me and said, *"Something you did offended me and I wanted you to know that I forgive you for offending me."* I had no knowledge of the offense and did not do anything intentionally to hurt him. In reality, it was an issue he was working through and had nothing to do with me. The real issue revolved around the authority figure that I represented in his life and what he had transferred onto me. Even though he walked away feeling better because he confessed it to me, I walked away feeling slimed. That is the reason we need to make amends in the arena in which the offense took place; otherwise, we risk creating a counter offense in the other person. However, if the offense is known by both parties, then it is best to go forgive and release that person.

Matthew 18:15-17 gives the general procedure to address the reconciliation of relationships. This passage seems to be in context of straightening out sins against each other in the church. In it there is an order to the steps to be taken in mending an offense. The passage tells us that the first step is to go to the offender in such a way that you are not backing him into a corner. (I believe that is why the Bible tells us to go to the person in private first.) However, if going to that person in private will subject you to further emotional wounding, you might need to skip that step and take someone else along with you. Keep in mind that you should not initiate this process of reconciliation if you aren't willing to carry it all the way through to the end.

Always keep in mind that the person with whom you carried the offense might not be at a place to restore the relationship. He or she may not be able to receive anything from you. Your objective is to set things straight with God first and to get free from the bondage of bitterness. Restoration of the relationship would be an added benefit, but not always possible. You are responsible to address your part in a wounded relationship. That is all God is asking you to do. If God leads you to pursue further restoration, then obey the Lord, but remember that it is not always necessary or possible to pursue that, though it may be preferable.

One of the questions that come up from time to time is the role of forgiveness towards those who may be prone to hurt you again. To this I would say that forgiveness does not mean that you should remove the proper boundaries that could prevent future damage. You do not lose your common sense when you forgive. Some wrongly assume that if forgiveness is given, everything should be restored to a prior original state.

I had a woman complain to me that her unfaithful husband was telling her that she had not forgiven him because she put boundaries around her emotions and still distrusted him. She came to me bothered by his complaints and asked me if she had truly forgiven him even though she had these boundaries intact. Her husband thought that if she had forgiven him, then everything should be as it was prior to the unfaithful behavior. To him, forgiveness meant they went back to what they were before the offense, and act as if the adultery had not happened. In reality, he was hoping to evade the consequences of his actions by putting the, *"I thought you forgave me"* guilt trip on her. She had, in fact, really forgiven her husband for his infidelity and was willing to be reconciled but trust was at an all time low! It was not that she did not forgive, as her husband perceived, but the pain of the offense had tenderized her heart so severely that she found herself having to work through her emotions of betrayal. Her actions were not designed to chastise him. They were to protect her heart from further wounding until trust could be rebuilt.

The offender could be a person who sexually molested you, a person who verbally belittled you, one who physically abused you, or one who betrayed you. If you have been wounded and the potential of further wounding is possible or even probable, boundaries are necessary. Forgiveness does not mean you release your boundaries and open yourself up to further abuse. Forgiveness does not mean you must now surrender to blind trust. Trust is something that is earned. If a person has violated trust, you can forgive him, but trust has to be rebuilt! You can forgive and still maintain good boundaries that prevent further wounding.

Chapter 4

The Bottom Line: What does forgiveness do for you?

Tim, a young man who went through this material on forgiveness as a requirement for his ministry school wrote me and told the impact of forgiveness had on his life. He said, *"I had never thought of forgiveness as canceling a debt, or getting rid of an expectation of someone owing me something. While I read the book the Holy Spirit started bringing up people and situations where I had never forgiven them. So I allowed the Holy Spirit to take me to those places and I forgave those people and canceled the debt that I thought they owed me. I noticed as well that when those situations occurred, the relationships I had with those people began to decline and I couldn't figure out why. Since forgiving those people, I have talked to two of them and the whole friendship has changed like a huge wall had been knocked down! IT IS AMAZING!!* One of my friends would sometimes back out of a meeting with me at the last second. This person also had a tendency not to call me back, usually 99% of the time. God showed me that I had never forgiven him for backing out and not calling me back. That friend called me within 48 hours after forgiving him, and I had not contacted him in months by phone!"

This is just one of many stories of how the spiritual climate over people changes when they forgive. The unseen world is altered whenever we do something that is in agreement with heaven. Angels are activated, demons become bound, and there is a shift in the atmosphere that is not always seen by the naked eye. Jesus said that we are given keys that bind and loose so that the gates of hell will not prevail. Our activities will release what has been bound and bind what needs to be released. Nothing seems to do this more than forgiveness. Healing is released in the body, division among people becomes mended, and heaven's favor is restored. The atmosphere around your life is changed and this shift can be felt by those around you. There will be something inviting about you that others just can't put their finger on, but they will know something is different.

Forgiveness is best for what it does for you. It enables you to move on with your life instead of keeping some areas on hold until someone apologizes or some event happens to fix the pain. You do not have to stay imprisoned or stuck because of bitterness. You can choose to forgive and be released from the chains of bitterness and be able to move on and start rebuilding your life. You are the one who benefits in forgiving others.

Not only does it benefit you, but it benefits others as well. How many in your life have felt the brunt of your anger because they unknowingly pulled a trigger and got "dumped" on? Do the people in your life walk around on egg shells because they don't want to accidentally light your short fuse? Are people leery of getting real close to you because they don't like getting the fallout of burning embers from a volcano explosion? It may not be that you had thought about spewing all over them. Instead, it is simply the residue of bitterness erupting from some unresolved past hurt that rose up momentarily and got a little out of control. It only takes a few seconds of spewing to erode years of building trust.

The result of forgiveness is the freedom to pursue the purposes of God for your life. In the book of Genesis is the story of Joseph. His brothers who had considered killing him ended up selling him into slavery. He wound up as a slave in Egypt and later on was falsely accused and tossed into prison. His brothers had horrendously sinned against him. Joseph encountered his brothers after God had freed and elevated him to the most powerful position in Egypt under Pharaoh. They were afraid of what Joseph would do to them because of how they had sinned against him. However, Joseph met them with mercy because of his love for them. Later after their father, Jacob, died, they again feared that Joseph would seek his revenge on them. And again, Joseph reassured them of his love by saying ... *"Do not be afraid, for am I in God's place? And as for you, you meant evil against me, but God meant it for good in order to bring about this present result, to preserve many people alive."* (Genesis 50:19-20)

Joseph was free to pursue God's destiny for his life because he had a heart to forgive. Once he rose to power, he wasn't devising revenge on his brothers now that he had the authority to do so, nor was he seeking to crush Potifer, who had put him in jail. He, instead, went about doing the business of God, unhindered by the treachery of others. Somewhere, he had a choice to make - either to hang onto the offense or to really let go of the offense. In his decision to let go and let love rule, he would be in a place that God could trust. From that place, God was able to entrust him with a great amount of authority because He knew Joseph would not abuse that authority. Joseph was free to do the will of God to preserve his brothers, the abusers, rather than destroy them. He was able to fulfill his destiny because he was not weighed down with bitterness.

Unforgiveness stifles God's destiny for our lives. It clouds our motives. It pollutes our purpose. It tempts us to deviate from our course. When unforgiveness is present, we find ourselves weighed down and easily worn out. When we have a heart that is willing to forgive, then the weights that hinder us are gone. When we forgive, we live in freedom – freedom is a great place to dwell!

Chapter 5

What if I don't want to forgive?

When we choose to bless others with what God has given us, we put ourselves in a position to receive a greater blessing. In blessing others we become blessed because what we give is returned to us many times. God's Word says, *"Give, and it will be given to you; good measure, pressed down, shaken together, running over, they will pour into your lap. For by your standard of measure it will be measured to you in return."* (Luke 6:38) We are recipients of the blessings of God when we give what we have been given. But the opposite is true also. Whatever we give out, whether good or bad, will be given back to us in greater proportions. That is the law of the harvest. We reap back what we sow, we reap later than we sow, and we reap more than we sow. So, we have a choice in what we reap; the effects of blessing or the effects of cursing. When we suffer the effect of a curse, the suffering is essentially the damage and ruin toward ourselves for not choosing to give what we have received.

We can receive God's love without giving it. We can receive mercy without giving it. We can receive God's forgiveness of sins without forgiving others who have sinned against us. When we do not give, we shut off the flow of grace from our lives. As a result, spiritual, emotional, and possibly even physical diseases are given permission to operate in us.

Let's not fool ourselves; there are consequences when we refuse to forgive. These alone should motivate us to forgive, but often times they do not. The Bible says that, *"God is not mocked; for whatever a man sows, this he will also reap."* (Galatians 6:7-9) There are consequences. However, do not forget that there are also great blessings that will flow to us if we sow into the Spirit. You can identify the seed of what you have been sowing by examining the fruit of the crop you are harvesting, both good and bad.

For one thing, does there seem to be a whole horde of "tormentors" that have been unleashed in your life. There is a story given by Jesus in Matthew 18 (verses 21-35) that describes this process. It is a story of a man who owed the king a huge amount of money so large that it was unpayable. When the servant asked for mercy, the king forgave the whole debt. The next thing that happened was that the servant came across a buddy who owed him a small amount. However, rather than forgive the small debt after he had been forgiven the huge debt, he decided to take his buddy to task. He choked him, demanded his small amount and eventually tossed his buddy in the slammer until the debt was paid. When the king found out what happened, he called the servant in and made him accountable for his actions. The result was that not only was the debt restored, but he was then tossed into the debtor's prison and there he was tormented by the tormentors. Another translation says that he was turned over to "torturers." (v. 34) I believe that the torturers are tormenting demons that take advantage of our lack of protection. When we have been forgiven by God for such a great debt and yet refuse to forgive others, our spiritual covering is blown. We are unprotected. We have chosen to walk out from under the protective umbrella. We become easy prey to the demonic realm.

Another thing that happens when we refuse to forgive is that we are cursing ourselves. We need to know that the tongue is a powerful force. It can bring blessing or it can bring cursing. James 3:8-10 says, *"But no one can tame the tongue; it is a restless evil and full of deadly poison. With it we bless our Lord and Father; and with it we curse men, who have been made in the likeness of God; from the same mouth come both blessing and cursing. My brethren, these things ought not to be this way."*

Whatever we send forth from our tongue is what we reap. Luke 6:38 (a verse we looked at earlier) is about "giving and receiving" in the context of judging one another. Whatever we send forth with our words returns to us. That is why we are told to "bless our enemies" and "bless those who curse you." (Luke 6:28; Romans 12:14) You may think you are getting revenge on another by speaking evil against that person, but you are actually hurting yourself more. It is like filling up a cup with poison for your offender and then drinking it yourself. You become poisoned by your words. Jesus said, *"For by your words you shall be justified, and by your words you shall be condemned."* (Matthew 12:37)

Another thing that I see often is that there are physical problems that develop. Your physical state is definitely affected by your emotional and spiritual state. That does not mean that every physical ailment is emotionally or spiritually related. However, there is more connection between these than many realize. Many physical problems have their roots in spiritual issues. If the root is spiritual in nature, then the only complete cure is to address the issue on a spiritual level. Otherwise, you have disease management instead of healing. Personally, I have seen more physical healing by working with people through the issues of forgiveness than any other method. If bitterness is at the heart of the physical problem, forgiveness is the primary cure.

James 5:15-16 implies a connection between sin and physical problems. It says, *"And the prayer offered in faith will restore the one who is sick, and the Lord will raise him up, and if he has committed sins, they will be forgiven him. Therefore, confess your sins to one another, and pray for one another, so that you may be healed. The effective prayer of a righteous man can accomplish much."*

One day I was meeting with a few leaders in our church for prayer when a lady came knocking on the door desperate for prayer. She was on disability retirement for her back and that day she was in so much unbearable pain that it drove her to come find us to pray. As we prayed, she wasn't getting any immediate relief. A question popped in my head regarding her husband so I asked her about him. She then told us the story about how he had deserted the family 25 years earlier. I then asked her if she had forgiven him. Her immediate response was to minimize its impact as she said, "Oh, it was a long time ago. I'm over it now." Then I responded, "So, you don't mind if I just lead you in a simple prayer of declaration to forgive him and release his debt to you?" You would have thought that I started sawing off her legs by the outburst of pain that followed. For the next ten minutes she vented her pain of how she had to eek out a meager living and raise her children alone while he was gallivanting around with other women and living a carefree life unencumbered by the burden of raising a family. He had plenty of funds to support his family but ended up blowing it on everything else instead. She retorted with, "He doesn't deserve to be forgiven! I will NEVER forgive him for what he did!" So much for being over it. Finally over a period of thirty minutes or so, we were able to show her the relationship between unforgiveness and her pain. We led her through forgiveness, prayed again for her back, and the Lord totally relieved her physical pain. I, myself, have witnessed countless people get physically healed, similar to this woman, when they chose to forgive an offender.

Once I was ministering with my wife in a church in Brazil. On one particular night we had a whole line of only women. The first lady comes up and talks about needing prayer for her back pain. As we prayed for her, the Lord led us to ask her about some men in her life who had wounded her. She confessed her anger and bitterness and when she forgave, her back pain left. The next woman comes up and she also had back pain. Again as we were praying for her, the Lord led us to address her bitterness towards a man. When she forgave him she was healed. After the first three, we began to see a pattern. It was really an unusual night because not only did they all have back pain, but they also had men in their lives who hurt them in some way. Every one of them was healed when they forgave their offender.

When a person is bound with bitterness, it seems that it often seeps its way into the bones and joints. I am not saying every person who has bone problems have it because they have deep bitterness, but it is something very possible that needs to be checked out.

Recently on a trip to South Africa, at the end of a meeting in a rural village church, one of the ladies on our team was praying for a woman who seemed to have a large number of physical ailments. After a long period of time, there just wasn't any progress. When I looked at her, I felt an impression that there was some unresolved bitterness. I approached her and blurted out without forethought, "Who is the man you need to forgive?" It was her husband who abandoned her years ago. That night she was totally healed within minutes of forgiving. A couple of days later when the participants were testifying to the grace of God in their lives, she shared how she was totally healed that night. The pain in her knees and her back was gone. Her hearing loss was restored. She had been on medication for tuberculosis for eight years and she went through the past two nights without any. She said that all the chronic physical ailments she had been struggling with for the past eight years were all gone!

Whenever you have bitterness against another, you can't receive the good things that God may want to impart to you through that person. It causes you to cut off any impartation of blessing that another has to offer. It is hard to receive anything from someone where there is an unresolved offense.

One common thing I see is when people have not forgiven their parents for wounding they received earlier in life. In that state of unforgiveness, they cut themselves emotionally from their parents, often vowing never again to relate to them or be like them. The effect is that you cut off your inheritance. Your parents, regardless of whether they were good or bad, have a source of blessing that is your rightful godly spiritual inheritance. Even though it is difficult to see it in some parents, there is blessing somewhere up the family line that we need to call down to ourselves. Bitterness puts a wall that shuts off any spiritual family inheritance because we simply can't receive. As a part of this same thing, we all have a masculine and feminine heritage that is passed on to us. Bitterness can shut it down and your vow can cut off what God would want passed on to you.

The same is true if you have bitterness against the pastor or a teacher in your church. There may be great amounts of blessing that can come from your spiritual leaders, but if an offense is there, your capacity to receive is greatly reduced. Great truths and great measures of blessings can be missed when offenses are present. Just look at the Gospels and see how the religious could not receive from Jesus because He offended them. With the enormity of truth that flowed from the mouth of the Messiah, the offended couldn't receive a word of it. They heard it, but they could not receive it. When I counsel someone who says to me, "I'm just not getting fed anymore," I look first to see if an offense is present. If the pastor or teacher had fed them spiritually in the past and now they do not, it might not be that the leader has lost their ability to teach, but that the person has lost their capacity to receive. Bitterness will do that. It will erode your capacity to receive even the great things that another can give and bless you with. You will find this in marriage that when you have bitterness against your mate, you will not receive the good that could come from your spouse.

Here's the clincher. Your offender still has power over you until you forgive. That ought to irritate you if nothing else does. You could be sitting around, angry as you can be, thinking that as long as you do not forgive, you are punishing your offender(s) while in the meantime your offender can be going about the activities of their daily routine enjoying themselves, not even thinking about you much less concerned about you, and going on with life. *But NO! You are punishing them, right?* Who is really getting punished?

In order to get a genuine reality check, as some are sitting in a counseling time or going through session after session of inner healing meetings going over the same stuff of unresolved bitterness, we have to ask, *What is your offender doing now? Are they bothered right now by what they did to you? Is your unforgiveness really disturbing them? Is your bitterness afflicting pain on them and causing them to suffer and paying them back because of what they did?* Usually the answer to those questions is, "No!" Hopefully they will wake up to see that something is wrong with this picture when they are the ones in the endless counseling sessions and their offenders aren't.

Chapter 6

How Bitterness Gets Embedded in a Heart

As unforgiveness is allowed a place to rule in your heart, you eventually allow the building of a stronghold of bitterness. The term, "stronghold" may not be a part of your everyday vocabulary but it would be helpful to understand this concept in light of the damage that unforgiveness brings to a person. A stronghold is an ingrained repetitive thinking process your mind regularly travels down. What you think determines how you see yourself, how you see others, and how you see your world. Right or wrong, what your mind and your thoughts gravitate to determine how you live and who you will become. Therefore, a stronghold is a dominating thought pattern that rules how you think, how you respond, and determines your behaviors. Strongholds can be either godly or ungodly. Your thought patterns can either bring you into life or bring you into ruin. Although I will talk more on developing a godly stronghold later on in this book, for now I want to focus on the negative side.

When an ungodly stronghold rules your life, you find yourself becoming a slave to your thoughts and those thoughts controlling you rather than you controlling your thoughts. When you have a stronghold of bitterness you have lost control of how you feel towards another person or situation. Since bitterness is nothing more than unfulfilled revenge, you stay angry or vengeful in your attitudes even though you might even act cordial on the outside. At this point, you have become enslaved to the bitterness, to the person, or to the situation. They have power over you. As long as you can't forgive, bondage prevails. Bitterness then becomes the personal damage that you do to yourself because you have chosen to either not forgive or feel powerless to forgive. When I use this term in this section, I am referring to a negative place that rules, controls, or dominates your thoughts and therefore dictates negative behaviors. You find this terminology in 2 Corinthians 10- *"For though we live in the world, we do not wage war as the world does. The weapons we fight with are not the weapons of the world. On the contrary, they have divine power to demolish strongholds. We demolish arguments and every pretension that sets itself up against the knowledge of God, and we take captive every thought to make it obedient to Christ."* (2 Corinthians 10:3-5 NIV) We engage in spiritual battle to tear down and demolish strongholds. These demonic strongholds are those ingrained thought patterns that are raised up against the knowledge of God and are disobedient thoughts that have yet to be taken captive. When unforgiveness rules, it gives way to further thoughts that are in direct opposition to the character of God and the will of God. When we do not address the areas of unforgiveness in our lives, those areas eventually become our master that determine how we think and feel. Even though we may succeed in temporarily putting resentment in the background of our minds, it still surfaces from time to time and its effect on our lives is still present.

It is important to understand that there is a process in which a stronghold is built. Strongholds are not built overnight, but over a period of time when we do not address an issue appropriately by letting grace rule in our hearts. All strongholds begin when we open a door and give the devil a place in which to operate. Ephesians 4:26-27 says, *"In your anger do not sin: Do not let the sun go down while you are still angry, and do not give the devil an <u>opportunity</u>."*

The word "opportunity" is defined as: *opportunity, power, place of operation, an area of legal control.* It refers to the first step in opening the door to yielding legal jurisdiction. It is also translated in many different ways. It is translated as *"foothold"* in the New International Version. The King James Version translates it as *"place"* while the New Revised Standard says, *"Do not make room."* The New Century Bible conveys the meaning as it translates the verse - *"Do not give the devil a way to defeat you."*

The devil wants a base of operation in our lives. Although we have protection by what Christ did on the cross on our behalf, we can still provide such a place if we choose to harbor sin. Once we surrender some real-estate in our hearts, the devil seeks to build on it. He doesn't rule the whole heart, only the block we let him move into. From there, a stronghold is methodically constructed until this structure of thoughts dominates our minds and is followed by behaviors.

A stronghold of bitterness starts off when we do not deal immediately with offenses. We open the door when we do not forgive and it becomes the devil's *opportunity*, his *foothold* because we gave him *room*. As long as we allow thoughts of unforgiveness in our heart, we are yielding our thought life to the kingdom of darkness. One thing is for sure – if we give the devil a foothold, he will build on it as much as we will allow.

At first we might be in control of how we feel, but later the feelings will rule us because we have opened the door to the lies of the devil. The demonic thoughts of blame, accusations, self-condemnation, and hate are given the legal right to dwell in our lives. Our demonic adversary wants to destroy our lives. He wants us to self-destruct with our own bitterness. However, the only way he can operate is to be given a right to operate. This defeated foe has lost all authority because Jesus destroyed his works by way of the Cross-where the kingdom of darkness was defeated, put to shame on the cross, and stripped of all their authority. Therefore, the only authority the devil has in our life is the authority we give him. He only has power when we empower him. Since he was completely and thoroughly stripped, he has to resort to deception to fool us into giving him our authority. We grant such permission and give him an "opportunity" or "foothold" whenever we believe the lies and refuse to forgive. These become inroads into our lives that, if left unresolved, will eventually bring us to a place of enslavement. At the point of enslavement, which I am calling a "stronghold," the thoughts of bitterness are so entrenched in our hearts and mind that we essentially become ruled by them. It is at this point that we can find ourselves helpless to forgive. It is best to be aware of these "opportunities" or "footholds" that open the door and give permission for a stronghold of darkness to become eventually built.

Retaining an offense rather than releasing an offense is the first open door. We have all been offended from time to time. If we were to probe this area and were asked: Has anyone ever betrayed you? Have you trusted someone who betrayed that trust? Has anyone said things about you that were intended to verbally wound you? Has anyone ever hurt you or done something that wounded you, physically or emotionally? Did your spouse ever desert you, have an affair, or refuse to show you any affection? Have you ever been fired from a job for no valid reason? Has a friend ever turned against you? We all have to admit that we have been offended from time to time. The question isn't, "Will you be offended?" but, "Will you retain the offense or release the offense?" The temptation is to choose not to forgive that person for their offense, but rather to hang on to it.

Next comes our response to the offense. This is where we often want to justify our retention of unforgiveness by saying, *"I have a right to be mad at that person!" "You don't know what that person did to me!" "I didn't deserve that kind of treatment!"*

Even though those are genuine feelings, the question still remains, will I choose to hang onto the offense, or will I choose to give it up.

We also open the door when we hang on to expectations that are not fulfilled. Regardless if that expectation is legitimate or not, realistic or unrealistic, if that expectation has not materialized, we are prone to be resentful and become bitter about it. Forgiveness will require you to release your expectations regardless of their legitimacy. When you do that, you may have to go into mourning as you will feel the loss and pain associated with cutting off unrealistic or simply unfulfilled expectations.

When counseling couples, it isn't uncommon to see a spouse who is angry at their partner for not fulfilling their expectations. Some of these expectations are like the conditions of a mutual agreement or an unwritten contract. In other words, both parties have an awareness of these expectations and there is at least some sort of admission to these expectations. However, there are times when one partner doesn't live up to their agreement. It's quite common in relationships. When one falls short of the agreement this failure becomes like a breach of contract. The obligation to fulfill their responsibilities becomes a debt that is owed to the other. This is a legitimate expectation and failure to pay the debt can become an open door for bitterness unless the debt is released. I am not saying that the legitimate expectation shouldn't be fulfilled nor am I excusing the person who should be doing what the couple agreed to. However I am saying that you cannot allow that person's inability to fulfill their obligation to rule your thoughts and life.

At other times the mutual agreement isn't really mutual at all but is more of a one-sided individual assumption or personal preference. Then it becomes more of a hidden contract on the part of one person. Sometimes a person doesn't even realize that they have expectations until it becomes violated. When this happens, the person with these expectations becomes angry when the other person doesn't do what they expect. This is really unfortunate because it is a one-sided ordeal. There could be one sided expectations related to parenting roles, the frequency of sex, the level of commitment to church, the cleanliness of the house, or how you pick up after yourself. The outcome seems to be the same whether the expectation is mutually agreed upon or just in the mind of one party. When the expectation doesn't happen, you might be able to tolerate it for a while. You might voice your expectation or you might even just keep it to yourself hoping it will happen without you saying anything. If those expectations are constantly violated then you must make a choice. You could either choose to allow that unfulfilled expectation to control how you feel and create bitterness in you, or you can recognize that you cannot control another person and therefore release your unfilled expectations. Again I'm not saying that these expectations aren't legitimate. However, if it looks like they will never be fulfilled, you must decide if you want to be ruled by another person's failure.

Another common area in which people must give up expectations is in relation to their parents. Maybe you have an offense against your parent because of the way they did not love you. Maybe they rejected you, abused you, or verbally wounded you. As a child, you have the "right" to be loved by your parents. It is their parental obligation to you to meet your needs and provide you with a loving home. You have a legitimate expectation for your parents to love you, demonstrate that love, and never abandon you. However, those expectations might never get met. They might be totally incapable of expressing appropriate love. You may always be stuck in a place of bitterness if your forgiveness is dependent on your parents somehow gaining the capacity to love you and fulfill your expectations. As you release those expectations to God, you will need to call on Him to meet the needs of what your parents could not do. In doing so you are taking back the power they currently have to hurt you. Only then can you choose to love without expecting anything in return.

Forgiveness acknowledges the expectation, but in turn, lets it go. This area is sometimes excluded on the topic of forgiveness because of the fact that this kind of offense rises out of the heart of the offended and not necessarily from an action of the offender. As long as we hang on to unfulfilled expectations, we are potentially subjecting ourselves to harbor resentment.

We can open doors when we entertain a lie and lies becomes embedded when we believe them. The progression could happen like this: an event occurs in which there is a wounding of the heart. It may have been an actual malicious action that wounded you, or you may have been hurt by your perception of the event as viewed through your filters. Either way, the kingdom of darkness was present to whisper lies into your mind that you received as truth. These lies could be things such as,

> "*They really don't care about me... They think I am worthless... I am not as loved as my sister (or brother)... They would rather be married to someone else than to me... God hates me... God only created me because He wanted someone to torment... They only want to destroy me... I have to punish them... There is no one else to hold this offense against them,*

so it is up to me... They don't deserve to be forgiven... Someone has to remember what they did..."

These thoughts may or may not have actual merit; however, it doesn't matter because they feel true to you. You may even mentally acknowledge them as lies, but they still feel true. Lies have nothing to do with reality. They are thoughts interjected into your mind, thoughts that you entertained and eventually believed. They became truth to you. The good news is that the Holy Spirit is able to help you see past the lies and embrace the truth. It's important to take some time and spend it with the Holy Spirit and allow Him to bring you into revelation.

When you refuse to forgive, because you have a "right" not to forgive, you not only give the devil a *place*, or a *foothold* in an area of your soul but you are now feeding it. Hebrews 12:15 says, *"See to it that no one comes short of the grace of God; that no root of bitterness springing up causes trouble, and by it many be defiled."* This verse tells us that we are to live in God's grace so that no root of bitterness can spring up. With the Lord, there is grace to forgive. When we live in God's grace, we live in the power to forgive where bitterness cannot take root. However, if the heart is fertile for offenses, the seed of an offense is planted in that fertile soil and it grows up. The effect is that others become defiled as well. I believe that one of the main ways we shut off the flow of grace is when we feel we are justified in retaining an offense. It comes when we feel we have the right to not forgive. The truth is, if you have received the grace of the Lord, you gave up your rights to retain an offense. Your choice to receive God's forgiveness is also your choice to release all your personal rights to hang onto bitterness.

Here's another problem. The longer you wait to forgive, the harder it is for you to forgive. The deeper a root grows, the more difficult it is to remove. Though nothing is impossible to God, He demands our cooperation for its removal. The deeper it grows, the more unwilling we become to let the Lord run deep in our lives. To make matters worse, what may reinforce those roots could be the inner vows we make that hold us in bondage such as, *"I will never forgive!"* When I say this, I'm telling myself that this is an indication that a stronghold of bitterness is already present. Sadly, I come across some from time to time who actually live out those inner vows to never forgive. They do not listen to reason and the door they opened has now turned into a full blown stronghold.

If bitterness remains then it seems to migrate to affect the whole person in other areas as well. Once a stronghold of bitterness is established, a negative support system of other bondage areas begins to rise up to reinforce it. Bitterness will pour into other areas and infect the other parts like a cancer. Many issues and problems in a person's life will have their root source in unforgiveness. Let's say a person has an inability to release offenses and therefore find themselves living in their hurts. The result is that they develop trust issues. They may then give themselves over to a fear of people and fearing close relationships they cripple any kind of emotional support system that would be helpful to them as they go through life. Another person who has been betrayed becomes filled with anger against another. Just thinking about the betrayer brings up uncontrollable anger thus more ground is given over. Someone else becomes verbally wounded by someone close. They take those words to heart and allow feelings of rejection to enter. The kingdom of darkness gains more ground through depression. Another person hurt by a spouse begins to look in other places to find attention or a sense of significance. He or she may seek attention from members of the opposite sex, yielding to the new ground of lust. Strongholds give ground to other areas. They build an active support system of thought patterns that can rule your mind and, ultimately, dictate your behavior.

On the one hand, if you do not have a relationship with Jesus, it is natural for you to be full of bitterness. The Bible describes it this way in Romans 3. It says *"As it is written, 'There is none righteous, not even one; There is none who understands, There is none who seeks for God; All have turned aside, together they have become useless; There is none who does good, There is not even one.' 'Their throat is an open grave, With their tongues they keep deceiving.' 'The poison of asps is under their lips'; **'Whose mouth is full of cursing and bitterness.'"** (10-14) Whenever a person who has not received God's grace tells me that they can't forgive, I believe them. They just can't help themselves. The power they are attempting to use is the power of the soul. Some are able to work it out in their minds and then choose to forgive, but most find themselves powerless to get past offenses. However this shouldn't be the case for those who have received God's grace.

Here is the truth. Since I have received God's grace of forgiveness, by forgiving others I can shut the door to the opportunities where the devil would want to occupy. I know that our adversary is a liar and a cheat. He will invade any place that will be opened to the kingdom of darkness. He thinks that any place of darkness in our lives gives him and the kingdom of darkness an opportunity to occupy. If I allow these opportunities to stay, then I am allowing the kingdom of darkness to build a whole structure of thoughts that will, literally, suck the life out of me. If I refuse to forgive, then I open the door for the "tormentors" to occupy and torment me. Thank goodness that I now have the power in Christ to choose to forgive!

CHAPTER 7

TEARING DOWN THE STRONGHOLD OF BITTERNESS

Are you ready to push your way into freedom and put your bitterness behind you? God has given you powerful weapons with which to tear down strongholds. (2 Corinthians 10:3-5) If you have unknowingly cooperated with building a stronghold of bitterness, the good news is that it can be unraveled so that grace can flow to bring liberty. The following steps are designed to assault the inroads of bitterness and dismantle them. Once dismantled and freedom is experienced, then the work of rebuilding a godly stronghold begins in order to sustain a heart that habitually forgives.

RECOGNIZE it for what it is: UNFORGIVENESS IS SIN.

The first step in ridding yourself of an area of bondage is to agree with how God sees it. *Recognition* means that you admit it and confess it to God. *Confession* means to come into agreement with God. You must see it as God sees it: SIN. What happens when you confess? 1 John 1:9 says, *"If we confess our sins, He is faithful and righteous to forgive us our sins and to cleanse us from all unrighteousness."*

Dear Lord, I acknowledge that when I choose not to forgive I am sinning against you. I have denied the power to forgive that you have given me through your Holy Spirit. You have forgiven me and in response to receiving your forgiveness, you ask me to forgive. I admit that I have not fulfilled my responsibility. I confess my sin of unforgiveness against you.

REVOKE the legal right for bitterness to remain: CHOOSE to forgive.

Bitterness remains because of a legal right. You hang onto the offense because you gave ground to it. You allocated a piece of the real estate in your heart to the offense and gave it a right to stay. When you open the door, the demonic strives to keep it open. The demonic are legalists. That's why they got along so well with the Pharisees. They attempt to enforce what legal right has been turned over to them. If you've opened the door, you have to close it and ask for the keys back. In this step you expose the lie that has kept you in bondage and remove the legal right for the bitterness to stay. You take back the ground you surrendered. You are, essentially, serving eviction papers to bitterness.

Ask yourself, *"What 'right' have I retained to not forgive that needs to be revoked? What 'inner vows' have I made? What 'lie' has the enemy embedded in my mind that keeps me from releasing the offense?"*

Now go to the Lord in prayer and take back the ground by praying through the following areas:

- Seek forgiveness for your part of the offense.
- Renounce your rights to not forgive.
- Renounce your inner vows to not forgive.
- Renounce the lie you have believed.
- Make a conscious choice to forgive, even if the feelings of forgiveness are not there.
- Release your offender into the hands of Jesus so that he or she will no longer have power over you.

REGAIN: Ask God to regain the surrendered ground that gave a "foothold" or "opportunity" for bitterness to take root.

Realize that God desires to bring restoration to the soul. Psalm 23:4 says that God, your Good Shepherd, restores your soul. You must deliberately ask Him to take back the ground given and to remove any bitterness. In this step you will be asking God to remove any right to go back and rekindle your bitterness.

This is significant because once the "right" to not forgive has been revoked and that ground is regained, you can no longer justify harboring resentment. Here is where so many of us get hung up. You want to forgive primarily because you know that is what you should do. However, to ask God to remove any right to rekindle bitterness sounds a little too permanent. To actually remove the right to harbor bitterness forces us to deal with our personal responsibility. You see, as long as you can blame others, you do not have to feel your shame. When justification to blame others is removed, then you have to look honestly with yourself.

In this step you are reinforcing the eviction notice. You are calling on God to uproot and boot out bitterness as an unwanted squatter. You are declaring that that piece of real estate has a new landlord, Jesus, and He's been given full authority over it. Nothing comes in unless it comes in through Jesus.

Dear Lord, your desire is that my soul be restored. I confess that I have given over legal ground for the adversary to set up camp in my life and build strongholds of bitterness. As I have confessed my sin to you and have revoked the legal right for the strongholds to stay, I ask you now to permanently take back the ground I have given over to bitterness. I ask you to remove any residue of bitterness in my life. I acknowledge that I am powerless to remove and take back the ground. I confess that nothing is impossible for you. I permanently surrender my right to hang onto unforgiveness. I surrender my right to blame anyone in order to stay bitter. Thank you, Jesus, for taking this ground back.

REMOVE the stronghold of bitterness and REPLACE it with God's truth.

Let's look again at 2 Corinthians 10:3-5. It says, *"For though we walk in the flesh, we do not war according to the flesh, for the weapons of our warfare are not of the flesh, but divinely powerful for the destruction of fortresses. We are destroying speculations and every lofty thing raised up against the knowledge of God, and we are taking every thought captive to the obedience of Christ."*

In these next few steps you are going to dismantle old thoughts and replace them with new ones. You are giving Jesus, your new landlord, remodeling rights over these regained areas. He wants to rip out the old structure so He can put in a new one. This old structure is destroyed only as you bring your mind into submission to God's Word. You are then able to confront the thought patterns that have ruled you and counter them with the truth and power of the Word of God.

Bitterness says, *"I must punish my offender."* The word of God says, *"Vengeance is mine, I will repay, says the Lord."* (Romans 12:19 is a great verse to commit to memory!) It is not your place to retaliate, but to allow the wrath of God to take its course.

As long as you withhold forgiveness, you are hanging onto your perceived right to punish your offender. It is never your job to punish your offender. That is always God's job. If you retain the sin and refuse to release it, then you are standing in God's way, hindering rather than helping, as God does His job. John 20:23 says, *"If you forgive the sins of any, their sins have been forgiven them; if you retain the sins of any, they have been retained."* You must assault that old thought pattern with the truth of God's Word. You must release your offender into the hands of God and declare that you have no right to bring retaliation.

When you take matters into your own hands in order to "get even" with your offenders, you miss out on the special blessing that God gives to those who choose to conquer by love. You also bring destruction to your own physical health, attitudes, and relationships.

Say out loud this declaration:

I declare that Jesus has defeated the powers of darkness by His shed blood on the cross. Satan and his demons have been stripped of all their power and authority by the death, burial, and resurrection of Jesus. The only power they have in my life is the power that I have given them, which I am taking back today. God has given me weapons empowered by His Spirit to tear down the lies that have kept me in bondage and any thought raised up against the knowledge of Him. I affirm the truth in God's Word. I declare that the Lord is my defender. Jesus is my righteous and just judge. I affirm that it is not my responsibility to avenge. It is Jesus' responsibility to bring justice to my offender, not mine. I declare that I will overcome through God's love working through me. I will be ruled by compassion, not my pain. I place my offender into the hands of Jesus who is my just judge and defender. I cut off any attachment I have to my offender and declare that he/she is now in the hands of Jesus.

REPENT of any false identity you have received from your offenders and REPLACE these with the truth of who you are.

Sometimes a person's life can be shaped by his or her offenders. You can turn into a person that isn't who you really are based on how others have related to you. In your hurts and wounds, you could develop unwanted behavioral patterns in how you relate to others. How you relate to people, how you react, how close you get to others are directly affected by how others have hurt you.

You might not be able to get close to others because you have established emotional walls around yourself. Or, you might gravitate to the other extreme and open yourself to everything and everyone with little regard to healthy boundaries because you want to be accepted and loved. You might have emotional reactions that have developed because of emotional wounding. You might have fears in certain areas that dominate you. The behavioral and emotional reactions can be so ingrained in you that you feel like that is who you are or who you have become, but that isn't true. Your true identity is not found in how you have been shaped by others. It is found in God who made you and in the freedom that you find in Christ. In getting free you may need to identify the areas you have embraced in your perceived identity that aren't the "real" you. These areas must be recognized as a false identity. Our true identity can be found in Christ. Therefore, you must let go by repenting of these false identities and embrace who you are in Christ.

One guy had a reputation of being a real trouble-maker. He had very few friends. He was seen as a person who was always angry and controlling. He liked to write letters to everyone giving them a piece of his mind. He was extremely opinionated and was closed to outside opinions. I didn't realize how widespread his reputation was or how bad a shape he was in. When I met him we butted heads right off the bat. He was argumentative and controlling. In that initial verbal altercation I told him that I didn't care whether or not he ever agreed with me and that my value didn't come from having his favor. However I was also able to communicate with him that there wasn't anything that he could do to make me dislike him. From that point on not only did the conversation change but the relationship changed. Unlike everyone else's experience with him, I always saw him as a great supporter and friend. I was able to see and know the real person. One of the older ladies in our church told me one time how amazed she was that it seemed like I had him doing whatever I wanted. In all of her years of knowing him, she had never seen him like this. He had become a controlling contentious person because of the things that he encountered in his youth. Growing up he had to become someone he wasn't just to survive, but that wasn't who he really was. He had learned to put up walls around his emotions and shut others out through controlling his environment and being extremely opinionated. He was one who was never wrong and argued his point to the extreme. What brought about the change in him was that he was able to enter into a relationship with someone who refused to carry an offense towards him and this changed the spiritual climate over him and brought him into a place of freedom. In this environment I was able to see who he really was rather than the contentious man he had become.

There was another woman who couldn't' seem to help herself in disagreeing with people. I think much of it is often done unconsciously. What happens is that inevitably when she's in a conversation with people she rarely can find herself agreeing with them. To agree would mean she would have to receive them so she always has to have something to disagree with. Trust issues are huge in her life. Because she is afraid of relationship she lives her life keeping people at arms length, often by offending them or being contentious. On one occasion I was able to see that she was a really warm and compassionate person. However, whenever her stuff got kicked up, no one comes too close. That isn't who she is, but that is who she has become.

Another woman lost herself in serving the church and serving others. It was great to get a lot of work done, but she did it so she didn't have to relate to people. Her bitterness had caused her to turn inward and find her value in activity.

Another woman was always negative and was an extreme pessimist. She was critical, judgmental, and never seemed to have anything positive to say. Needless to say, people didn't like being around her but she didn't have a clue why. Those in her family walked on egg shells for fear of being the brunt of her negativity. Her attitude came after her husband passed away and left her to raise the kids on her own. Others could talk about how pleasant she was before, but unresolved anger at her loss shaped her to be who she wasn't.

You might really be a caring person but because you've been hurt, you have shut that part of your heart down. You might really be friendly, but offenses have made you guarded and apprehensive about letting people in. Offenses may have caused you to be more cautious and fearful, rather than courageous and bold. The real you may want relationships, while the wounded heart avoids people. You may consider yourself a critical person or judgmental in nature. However, that isn't who you are, but, rather, that is what you have embraced.

For this step you are going to have to think it through and let the Holy Spirit bring you revelation. It might be helpful to take a sheet of paper and make four columns similar to the following chart. List the person, the offense, and then the false identity. The false identity can be: how you see yourself, a reaction you have, a fear you possess, a struggle you have in relating to others, a wall that you set up to protect yourself, an ungodly lifestyle you have, a negative tendency in your character, a sin you gravitate to, or anything else you have taken ownership of because of the offenses of others. As you list the offenders and their offenses, make sure you have released them in forgiveness. Confess to God your part in taking on this false identity. Repent and renounce that false identity and then declare your true identity of who you really are in Christ! Write out the truth regarding who God says you are!

Offender	Offense	False Identity	True Identity

Chapter 8

Rebuilding the area with a Godly stronghold of Compassion.

Anytime you tear down an ungodly stronghold, you never leave that ground unoccupied. You must now build a godly stronghold to replace the ungodly one that was just torn down. Do not leave the area vacant; you need to rebuild and remodel. When the house is swept clean, you do not leave it unoccupied. If the house isn't filled up, the potential to return to bitterness is great and the latter condition will be worse than the previous one. (Matthew 12:43-45)

When you rebuild with a godly stronghold, you rebuild in the opposite spirit. If you tear down an ungodly stronghold of pride or self promotion you must rebuild with a stronghold of humility. If you tear down an ungodly stronghold of self hate, you must rebuild with self love that is not self promoting but one that enables you to love your neighbor as you love yourself. Rejection is replaced with acceptance, lust and greed is replaced with contentment, hate is replaced with love, fear with trust, depression with joy, anxiety with peace, rudeness with kindness, and so on. This is a principle for living in freedom and necessary in order to renew the mind and change of the heart. The truth of God's Word must rule your thoughts and cleanse your heart. This is the key to keeping the door shut to darkness! This is the key to staying free!

In my opinion, here is where so many writings regarding forgiveness seem to really fall short. In fact this has to be one of the primary reasons I wrote this book. Most treatments of this topic focus on the process of forgiveness, not sustaining it. To me it seems to bring people to a point of addressing the priority of forgiveness but then stops without giving any tools to keep your freedom. How frustrating!

Building a righteous stronghold of compassion will give you power to sustain forgiveness and stay free. Bitterness causes you see a person through the eyes of anger. You want to reject them, keeping your distance. You don't want to love them or have any affection for them. You cringe at the thought of carrying any warm feelings for them at all. So what's the opposite of that? It's compassion. Compassion requires you to feel God's love for them and see them through His eyes rather than yours. It is to see their value and significance to Him. Bitterness wants the worst for someone. Compassion wants the best for them. Bitterness carries an inner anger but compassion carries an inner love. I know that the thought of building a stronghold of compassion where you have torn down bitterness sounds repulsive to many. However it is the key to living in freedom. When compassion rules you are not ruled by the thoughts of what they did, how you can get even with them, or how they should be punished. That baggage has been lifted off of you.

Building a godly stronghold requires giving time and attention to not only dismantle unwanted thought patterns, but to renewing the mind to building godly thought patterns. Building strongholds don't come automatically, but through intentional time and attention. Your job is to crowd out what you don't want and fill yourself with what you do want. You must remember that what you feed grows and what you starve dies. If you feed bitterness, it grows and compassion is quenched. If you feed compassion and quit feeding bitterness, compassion will rule your heart and bitterness will wither away. The next question should be about how that is accomplished. There are some things that you can do to starve bitterness and feed compassion.

Acknowledge God's Will To Forgive.

Just as you started the previous steps with recognizing unforgiveness to see it as God sees it, so you must begin the rebuilding process with an acknowledgment that if you want to obey God, you have no other choice but to forgive. Your choices are: obey God or rebel against Him. Ephesians 4:31 says, *"Let all bitterness and wrath and anger and clamor and slander be put away from you, along with all malice."* You must remind yourself that obedience to God's will is always for your own good. You always benefit through obedience.

Think about this passage from Jesus' Sermon on the Mount: *"You have heard that it was said, 'Eye for eye, and tooth for tooth.' But I tell you, do not resist an evil person. If someone strikes you on the right cheek, turn to him the other also. And if someone wants to sue you and take your tunic, let him have your cloak as well. If someone forces you to go one mile, go with him two miles."*

(Matthew 5:38-41 NIV)

When you look at this passage, what responsibilities were placed on the offended? He told them to turn the other cheek, to give away his tunic as well when sued, and to carry the burden an extra mile. Each of those situations has potential for harboring bitterness. When you look at the potential offender, Jesus doesn't address their responsibilities in the offense. It may seem unfair to us to place the burden of forgiveness on the offended, but Jesus did. He didn't place it on us to torment us but rather to free us. In that Matthew 5 passage, a heart that is protected against offense is presented. It seems that a heart of giving and submission keeps you in a place that shields you against bitterness.

Meditate On God's Forgiveness For You.

I do not know anything that really builds a heart of compassion like this one. When you drill a well by thinking about the great measure of God's grace towards us, compassion can't help but flow from it whenever you pump it. I have noticed that meditation isn't emphasized much these days though it is mentioned repeatedly in the Bible. (Joshua 1: 8, Psalm 1:1-3) People are reluctant to practice this essential discipline, perhaps, because of the association with New Age philosophy and practices. However, meditation is necessary to saturate your heart with truth. It takes time to repeatedly go over the same passage of scripture to draw out every ounce of insight possible.

Meditation is dwelling on a scripture or truth, chewing on it as you would chew on a stick of gum, and letting it sink into your heart. This is a new discipline for most and it ought to be emphasized more in church life. To build a stronghold of compassion, you need to spend time meditating on God's forgiveness for you. Earlier I mentioned a story on Matthew 18 about the man who owed the king more than he could pay (see verses 18:21-35) but after he forgave him of his enormous debt, he refused to forgive his buddy who owed a small amount in comparison.

A question that used to bother me in this passage about the man who was forgiven by the king was, *"Why was this guy unable to forgive his fellow servant?"* His debt was literally in the millions in today's dollars, too large to ever possibly repay; yet he could not forgive a small debt. If you recall the story, you will notice that the king forgave the whole debt rather than just lowering it. Why? Because it was unpayable! The king could have cut it in half, but it would still be too large to repay. He forgave it all in the way God forgives all our sin, not just a part of it. I feel the reason he could not forgive the small debt is that he never saw what he actually owed. The amount was so huge that he could not comprehend it. It was too great; to him it was some vague astronomical figure. He never really comprehended the value of what he actually owed. It was as if the money was in a vault in some far off land and he only saw the bank statements. If he could have gone into the king's bank vault and seen stack after stack of money, if he could have run his hands through pile after pile of gold coins in the amount of his debt, and then be taken to a table to see the handful of money that was owed to him, the comparison could have been made. Perhaps it would have made a difference. If the servant had seen the debt that he was forgiven of, he might have forgiven his fellow servant's debt.

We have difficulty forgiving because we have not seen our own true debt – the debt that nailed Jesus to the cross where He endured that agonizing death. We have not seen our sin the way God sees it. We have not seen what we were actually forgiven of.

Many of us were saved when we were young or in a stage of life that society would consider quite moral. Many of us never lost everything because of habitual sin. We may have done things we are ashamed of, but if we compare our lives with others, we may not have considered ourselves as bad a sinner as some. We shouldn't be comparing ourselves to others, but to God's standard of righteousness. In His light, the darkness of our sin and even the filthiness of our own righteousness (Isaiah 64:6) confront us and cannot be denied.

We can see another person's debts better than we can see our own. Though we need to see the great measure of our debt, it often seems hidden from us. We've never fully seen what we owed God because of our sin. God reveals our debt so He can reveal His awesome provision. He doesn't reveal the wickedness of our hearts so that He can beat us up and fill us with self-condemnation. He doesn't do it to remind us of how good He is and how bad we are, nor to remind us how undeserving we are. He reveals our debt and His payment in order to reveal the greatness of His love. Seeing the greatness of His love arouses in us a desire to walk in righteousness. The benefit of such a revelation is that our hearts are prepared to forgive others.

Think about it, why do we continue to sin? One reason is that we have not seen the effect of our sin on the Lord. We did not see the agony of Jesus on the cross. We weren't there to see that brutal sacrifice. If we could see the payment, we could see the debt. We continue to sin flippantly because we have not seen our debt in comparison with His provision.

Do you remember the story of the woman who came and washed Jesus' feet with her hair? (Luke 7:36-50) The Pharisees were repulsed by this sinner who was touching Jesus. She wept as she anointed and kissed Jesus' feet. As Jesus discerned their offended thoughts, He proceeded to tell them a story... *"Two people owed money to the same banker. One owed five hundred coins and the other owed fifty. They had no money to pay what they owed, but the banker told both of them they did not have to pay him. Which person will love the banker more?"* Simon, the Pharisee, answered, *"I think it would be the one who owed him the most money."* Jesus said to Simon, *"You are right."* Then Jesus turned toward the woman and said to Simon, *"Do you see this woman? When I came into your house, you gave me no water for my feet, but she washed my feet with her tears and dried them with her hair. You gave me no kiss of greeting, but she has been kissing my feet since I came in. You did not put oil on my head, but she poured perfume on my feet. I tell you that her many sins are forgiven, so she showed great love. But the person who is forgiven only a little will love only a little."*

The Pharisee's sin was as bad as the woman's, but because of the Pharisee's pride, God was actively against him. In contrast, the woman found mercy. She knew her debt, but the Pharisee was blind to his.

It is easy to be like that Pharisee and never see our debt. We can take God's mercy, which is His unmerited favor, for granted. Through His mercy we receive what we do not deserve. We can know intellectually the debt we owe without having actually "seen" it. Therefore, we need the Lord to give us a fresh revelation of our debt and of His mercy.

Our hearts would say, "*They don't deserve to be forgiven.*" The truth of God's Word is, *neither do we!* Because we have been forgiven much, we can forgive much. We need a fresh revelation of how much God has perfectly forgiven us. To build a godly stronghold of compassion, we must meditate on God's forgiveness toward us.

Begin accumulating passages of scripture to start meditating on relating to God's awesome forgiveness. To jumpstart you in that process, some scriptures to begin with are: Psalm 51; 85:2; Romans 5:15-19; Colossians 2:13, 14; and Hebrews 9:15.

Receive The Grace To Demonstrate Mercy Just As God Has Shown You Mercy And Forgiven You.

God desires to demonstrate mercy to us. Even though we deserve consequences because of our sin against God, mercy means that God chooses to release us from those consequences. You do not show mercy because someone deserves it. You choose to give mercy because you have received God's mercy.

Earlier, grace was defined as the unmerited inexhaustible power supply that flows from God to us and through us to do His will. Grace is closely associated with mercy in that it is available based on God's choice to give it, not on your merit to receive it. Receiving grace means that you have God's power available to you to forgive and show mercy.

God's grace is available to all who will receive it. As you have received the grace of God you are empowered to forgive. *"...bearing with one another, and forgiving each other, whoever has a complaint against anyone; just as the Lord forgave you, so also should you."* (Colossians 3:13)

Declare out loud:

Lord, You have shown me mercy and forgiven my sins against You. You have given me the grace to show mercy to others, I receive Your power to show mercy as You have shown me mercy. I can do all things through Jesus who strengthens me.

Love With The Lord's Love.

If you know the Lord, you have His love in you. His love isn't dependent upon someone loving Him in return. It is perfect. This is the kind of love He imparts to us through His Spirit. You can walk in that love when you walk in the Spirit. First John tells us, *"We know that we have passed out of death into life, because we love the brethren. He who does not love abides in death... Beloved, let us love one another, for love is from God; and everyone who loves is born of God and knows God. The one who does not love does not know God, for God is love. By this the love of God was manifested in us, that God has sent His only begotten Son into the world so that we might live through Him. In this is love, not that we loved God, but that He loved us and sent His Son (to be) the propitiation for our sins. Beloved, if God so loved us, we also ought to love one another."* (1 John 3:14, 4:7-11) God would not ask us to love like He does if it weren't possible. When we receive His love for us, we become infused with a love from above that is far beyond what this world offers. We become empowered to love with God's love. It is a love that does not require a love in return. It is a love that overshadows the sins of others and becomes the dominant ruling force in life. Love covers a multitude of sin. His great limitless love can manifest itself through limited humanity.

One of the issues we have with those who offend us is that we want them to either demonstrate some remorse or take the first step in making amends. However, God doesn't treat us that way. God's love initiates forgiveness. He took the first step for us. The Bible says, *"When we were unable to help ourselves, at the moment of our need, Christ died for us, although we were living against God...*

But God shows his great love for us in this way: Christ died for us while we were still sinners." (Romans 5:6, 8 NCV)

For the restoration of a relationship to take place, there must be some repentance and remorse. However, you may never see any repentance or remorse on the part of your offender. Your choice to forgive cannot depend on his or her actions; it must be based upon God's love ruling your heart. Granting forgiveness is a choice that you make regardless of the response you will get.

Remember that to love is to feel pain. Jesus felt the pain of betrayal and still chose to love. He loved his betrayer Judas. He loved Peter who denied him. He loved those who accused him and put him up on the cross as He petitioned, *"Father, forgive them for they don't know what they are doing."* Those are words of love.

You might ask, *"How can I love someone I don't trust? How can I love someone who is untrustworthy?"* God does! He loves you! If you want to be like Him, you will learn to love unconditionally as well.

If love is present, you will be grieved by the betrayal. That grief will lead you to prayer. It will lead you to intercede for the other person. You will go to God as Jesus did and say, *"Father, forgive them..."*

When there is love, there is forgiveness and there is no record kept of wrongs. For *"...Love...keeps no record of wrongs."* (1 Corinthians 13:5 NIV) However in light of that, love does not mean you throw out common sense when dealing with untrustworthy people. Love does not mean you can cast the precious pearls before swine to be trampled underfoot. Love does not mean you give responsibility without proof of faithfulness. When you are faithful with little, then you are put in charge over more. Love does not mean you give responsibility to those who can't handle it.

Responsibility is given to those who have proven their character and their faithfulness, and more responsibility is given as they continue to do so. Loving others does not deny that they must prove their faithfulness before you entrust them with certain responsibilities. Human trust has a weak and frail foundation because it will be violated by weak, frail, imperfect, sinful people. In contrast, love is not determined by whether a person is worthy or trustworthy. We love out of our debt to God. We cannot stay offended in such a great love.

Love requires you to ask God to help you see your offender through his eyes. This needs to be a conscious choice on your part. It needs to be a prayer request that stays on your petition list. It reminds you daily that eyes of compassion come only from God. It should push you to see God's perspective of man. God looks at you with eyes of love, a love that does not require an equal response, and He wants you to have His eyes and see others as He sees them. If you use a prayer list, take it out right now and add, *"God, help me to see _____ through Your eyes."*

Love requires you to erase any record of wrong daily. In the Lord's Prayer, we are encouraged to daily forgive as we pray, *"And forgive us our sins, for we ourselves also forgive everyone who is indebted to us."* (Luke 11:4, Matthew 6:12) This is the effect of God's love residing in you. As mentioned above, true love keeps no record of wrong. To build a stronghold of compassion means you make a practice of forgiving and erasing the record of wrongs you suffer from others. That does not mean that you do not use wisdom in relating to others who have offended you. However, it does mean that you do not let those past wrongs suffered rule how you relate to people; instead, you let God's love rule your relationships. Today have you erased the record of wrongs that have been committed against you?

To love with God's love means realizing that His love is already in us. We just need to exercise it to activate it. Maybe you need a little help in getting a "jump start" in loving with God's love. You might want to warm up to this idea with a little less threatening exercise. Start by thinking of a person whom you can love, but who is not in the habit of loving you. It does not require much to love when you are loved, so choose someone with whom you can practice loving with God's love, even if love is not returned. Start with a person with whom you don't have an issue. That person is much safer than trying to love the one who actively hates you. Start doing acts of kindness without expecting something in return to demonstrate God's love. The objective is to begin to establish habits of loving in God's way. In doing so you are training your heart to love.

Determine To Forgive Before An Offense Occurs

Since you know it is God's desire to forgive, you must determine that you will forgive before an offense happens. This is a lifestyle choice. This was the point in Jesus' conversation with Peter in Matthew 18:21-22. *"Then Peter came and said to Him, 'Lord, how often shall my brother sin against me and I forgive him? Up to seven times?' Jesus said to him, 'I do not say to you, up to seven times, but up to seventy times seven.'"* I'm sure Peter thought he was being quite generous in that suggestion. After all, seven is a great number and if you have forgiven another seven times, then it seems that you should have been able to fulfill your obligation. Jesus' answer I'm sure took Peter by surprise. Jesus tells him to forgive continually. How many people in our lives do we have at least four hundred and ninety (70 x 7) offenses to work through? I think Jesus is referring to a lifestyle and that means forgiveness should be something that is continually practiced and chosen.

Jesus modeled for us the ultimate demonstration of forgiveness in Luke 23:34 because of His compassion. Again we can point to the time that Jesus was hanging on the cross and down and said, *"Father, forgive them; for they do not know what they are doing."* The only way you could forgive in the way that Jesus did is to determine you will forgive, even before an offense occurs.

God wants you to become unoffendable. Jesus would say Matthew 5:38-39, *"You have heard that it was said, 'Eye for eye, and tooth for tooth.' But I tell you, Do not resist an evil person. If someone strikes you on the right cheek, turn to him the other also."* If you will approach life with this attitude, you can break the endless cycle of hurt and unfairness that can be so disabling.

It is quite likely that sometime tomorrow someone will offend you. It might even happen before this day is finished! It could be a co-worker, someone on the freeway, a store clerk with a bad attitude, a family member, or a telephone sales call. Why not begin your day with prayer asking God for grace to forgive for the times you will be offended that day?

Chapter 9

How About Those Lingering Feelings Of Unforgiveness?

Feelings are not always the best gauge of whether or not you have forgiven someone. Feelings change from day to day and are dependent on many different factors, from something chemical in your body to reacting to events around you. Feelings may be a reaction to old mental tapes you might be playing, or you might be responding to a relationship gone bad. Feelings come and go and are not always reliable; however, if feelings of unforgiveness continue to surface, review the forgiveness process to see if you have thoroughly worked through your portion.

Some people come back to me after a period of time and say that those feelings of unforgiveness have returned. Usually my first question is this, *How actively are you pursuing a stronghold of compassion?* Most have had to admit that building a stronghold of compassion was a little more work intensive than they anticipated. They preferred to have a quick fix and wanted to do as little as possible. Nevertheless, to complete the forgiveness process, it is imperative that you rebuild the area with a stronghold of compassion. This will take WORK and TIME! You will sabotage your wholeness if you do not do your part in pursuing compassion for those who hurt you.

I believe this is really the key to moving on and getting on with life. In many of the materials I have read relating to forgiveness, most do not even consider a rebuilding step. It is absolutely IMPERATIVE to fill the house with a "godly stronghold" once you've torn down an "ungodly stronghold."

Not only must you make sure you are building a stronghold of compassion, you must also insure that you are not entertaining any lies that are distorting your perspective. Woundedness can be grounded either in truth or in the perception of truth. Either it actually happened to you, or it was self-inflicted by your perceptions or expectations of the event. If it is a perception or twisting of the truth, then it is a lie that the adversary planted in your heart to disable you. To move on with your life and not be dominated by the emotions related to the wounding, you must remove any lies the enemy is using to keep you in bondage. If the wounding was self-inflicted because of perceptions or expectations, you must replace those thoughts with truth. These lies could include statements such as: *"No one really loves me,"* or, *"I have no worth or value."*

Thoughts could be person specific such as: *"Jim doesn't think I have worth or value,"* or, *"Fred doesn't love or like me."* The lie associated with such statements would be things like: *"My worth is dependent on what Jim thinks,"* or, *"I need Fred to love me to feel loved."* These statements can be dominant in those who are working through issues with parents and individuals to whom they have transferred their parental issues.

Lies that must be exposed and replaced with truth may sound like: *"I can't be free until I'm reconciled to my offender,"* *"My unforgiveness continues to punish my offender,"* *"I'm still in control when I don't forgive,"* or, *"My offender must repent and feel remorse for me to forgive."*

Take some time and see if there are any lies still resident in your heart that keep feelings of unforgiveness active. Ask God to search your heart thoroughly and expose any of the lies that still may be embedded there. *"Search me, O God, and know my heart; Try me and know my anxious thoughts; And see if there is any hurtful way in*

me, And lead me in the everlasting way."
(Psalms 139:23-24)

These thoughts need to be uprooted and exchanged for truth. Write down any lies that still have power over you. Write down the truth that confronts those lies.

As the lies are revealed and the truth comes forth, you must renew your mind and affirm the truth of your actions. Romans 12:2 says *"And do not be conformed to this world, but be transformed by the renewing of your mind, that you may prove what the will of God is, that which is good and acceptable and perfect."*

Remember that forgiveness is an act of the will, not an emotion. Emotions come later. You forgive as an act of obedience. Forgiveness involves releasing the offender to the Lord. *"By God's grace I choose to forgive you for the things you did to me. I release you from the anger and bitterness that I have held against you."* As the feelings of unforgiveness continue to rise, you submit them to the choice of forgiveness and bring them into submission. When you do that and pursue a stronghold of compassion, you will find that the feelings of forgiveness will prevail. As the mind is renewed, the emotions and feelings of forgiveness will come later. Many think that because the feelings of unforgiveness continue to rise, they have not forgiven the offender. That simply isn't true; emotions can change from day to day. Once you go through the process of releasing your offender, you must renew your mind with the truth that you forgave. In time, as you consistently continue to bring your mind in alignment with your choice to forgive, the emotions follow.

Speaking of emotions, have you released the emotions that were tied up with the offense? Emotions surrounding the offense may still be capped; you may have never expressed them or allowed yourself to feel them. They may be like a corked soda bottle that has been shaken and is now ready to spew. There are a couple of practical ways to release this inner tension without sliming everyone around you.

First, it may be helpful to write a letter to your offender. Express the hurt and pain you have felt. Say everything in the letter you have wanted to say to that person. Do not hold anything back. When you are finished, take that letter and permanently destroy it. Expressing all that you could not say before often brings emotional release.

Second, you could physically release the tension. I know some will disagree with me and others may wonder if I have really lost it with this next suggestion! Perhaps I have, but I have known a few who have ridden themselves of some inner tension this way, and as a result, I do not discard it, even though this would be my last resort. Take a baseball bat or a stick and pound the daylights out of a bed or a tree. Do not hold back feeling the anger, but let every bit of anger come up and feel it. This may have been bottled up for years and, to move on, you might need to express it physically. Perhaps while going through the forgiveness process, you never allowed yourself to feel the inward anger. Do not feel guilty about having feelings and expressing them. There is nothing wrong with having emotions or expressing emotions. God made you a person filled with feelings and emotions. We need only to take care of **how** and **where** we express our emotions so as not to slime others in the process!

Chapter 10

Forgiving Myself And Forgiving God

We know we need to forgive ourselves when we are overwhelmed with guilt and self-condemnation. What are you still beating yourself up with? In what areas do you feel you still need to suffer? If you feel as though you need to suffer some more or pay for what you've done, then you need to go through a good heart cleansing and let the Lord give you a clean conscience.

It's not uncommon to find people who beat themselves up or blame themselves for things that happened in their life. You might even deserve the blame but you can't live there. Self-pity and self-condemnation will cause a person to stay disabled. It is as if you feel like you need to punish yourself a little more then after you have suffered a sufficient amount of pain, then you can reenter the world. There is the natural cause and effect of our actions, but don't forget what Jesus died and paid for. He also paid for your sin against yourself. That's covered by His blood as well.

As you spend time with the Lord, let Him bring to mind what He wants you to repent of, not what you feel guilty for. Then confess to God your failure. When you confess, claim the promise of 1 John 1:9 that God will forgive and cleanse you. Next is the difficult part – receive God's forgiveness. This is usually more difficult because of the accusations of the enemy that come storming in and telling you that you are unworthy of such forgiveness. When that happens, address those thoughts and rebuke them, for they are not your own. They are thoughts put into your mind by the kingdom of darkness to keep you in defeat. Tell those thoughts to leave in the authority of Jesus. You have been bought with a price, you belong to the kingdom of light, and Jesus, alone, determines your value. This value is determined by what one is willing to pay. Jesus gave His life for you, and that is your value! Your debt has been paid in full. Just as you received Jesus into your heart by faith for salvation, you receive God's forgiveness by faith for cleansing of the heart.

Pray out loud:

Father, in the Name of Jesus I forgive myself for my sins against me. I renounce self-condemnation and self-judgment for the things that You have already forgiven me of because I have sincerely confessed them to You. I declare that the payment for my sin has been perfectly satisfied once for all by Jesus' sacrifice on the cross. I receive Your forgiveness and ask You to cleanse my heart. I ask You to help me discern between the conviction of the Holy Spirit for my sin against You and self-condemnation that I would heap on myself. Thank you Jesus that my value doesn't come from this world but comes from You. Amen

Though some know up front that they are angry and bitter against God, with others it is not that clear. Just as it is difficult for some people to admit being offended or angry at another person, some find it even more difficult to admit they are angry at God. I have heard people say, *"I can't be angry at God. He's God!"* Yet, in their hurt and expectations of Him, they are exactly that – angry at God. If this is you, He already knows you are angry with Him. He needs you to be honest with your feelings in order for Him to set you free.

Anger or resentment against God usually comes because we have an unfulfilled expectation of God. We do not understand how an all-powerful being would allow such suffering and pain. We do not understand how a God who claims to love can allow unloving things to happen. We have these expectations because we project onto God what we feel He should do to fix the situation. We want God to be codependent and to fix everything and do not understand why He does not. We may see God as some sort of Santa Claus who gives us what we want, or we may want God to be a loving grandfather type who spoils us.

If we have experienced wounding by people in authority, we may come to perceive all earthly authority figures as abusive and untrustworthy. Trust can be damaged because you misplaced it by trusting someone to do something that they failed to do, or to be someone that they refused to be. Once trust is violated, it is more difficult to trust the next time around. Our issues with people in positions of authority may be the result of having been hurt and abused by one or more of them. We might even project our fears and distrust onto God, the ultimate authority.

Offenses against God are on our part, not God's. God is perfect in every way, especially in how He relates to us. He does no wrong and has no sin. It is always our perspective that is warped when we have an offense against God.

God always looks beyond the present and makes decisions regarding our lives based on how we will spend our eternity. We have to understand that He is interested in getting us as prepared as possible for eternity. In our finite minds we can't see that far. We only see the present. Because His perspective is perfect, there are some things that He causes to happen. There are other things He chooses to allow to happen. Either way, God is still in control. God's plan for our lives includes pain and suffering as He prepares us for a glorious future. James 1 tells us to consider it all joy "when" we encounter various trials, not "if". We often do not understand this because we do not see the big picture of His plan for us.

A part of the devil's plan is to speak lies into our minds against God so that we will carry an offense against Him. As noted earlier, it is hard to receive from those against whom we carry an offense. If the devil can cause you to be angry at God, you are less likely to trust God. Anybody that has an offense against God has fallen prey to that attack and has listened to and believed the lies of the devil. If you are bitter at God, you may have allowed those demonically induced thoughts to have a place in your thinking.

The result of believing untruths relating to God is that trust is eroded. Trust is necessary to a deep and abiding relationship with God. It is the doorway to intimacy with Him. That is why the devil works hard to destroy it. What we do know about God is that He will never fail you. He is the only one who will never let you down. He is the only one who is trustworthy. Regardless if that feels true at times, it is truth. The integrity of our loving Father is always intact. Actually, God alone is worthy of our complete trust. Proverbs 3 says to, *"Trust in the Lord with all you heart and don't lean on your own understanding."* (v.5) When the world, people, and circumstances betray you, desert you, and condemn you, the only stable unchangeable One in your life is God. When you don't understand, you can always trust God.

Even though the issues we have with God are still our issues since God cannot sin against us, we sometimes still need to work it through. We may not be at a place where we can turn away from any unjustified anger against Him. We might not be able to admit our shortsightedness and release our self-imposed expectations of God. Ultimately we will need to come to that place where the lies we believed about God will need to be exposed and confronted so that the power of darkness has no power over you and the scheme to disable you from drawing power from your Creator is thwarted. We will eventually need to look past the self-inflicted offense and see God's hand for the greater good. However, until we come to those realizations of truth, we might only be able to get there through working through our offenses against Him and forgiving Him by releasing Him from any expectations we have put on Him.

I know this about God. God is never offended at our offenses against Him. Regardless of how we feel about Him, He always feels love towards us. God is filled with love and mercy. He never rejects you. You can be open and honest with Him in how you feel. His shoulders are broad enough to take anything you can dish out and still love you unconditionally.

Chapter 11

The Final Word

Forgiving the offenses of others may seem an impossible task, but it is the will of God. Everything that is in the will of God is backed up with the power of God. He will not command you to do anything without supplying the necessary power and the grace that you need. (Philippians 4:13)

No one said it would be easy. It will take your volition to choose to forgive. It will take tenacity to renew your mind when feelings of unforgiveness resurface. You will need to strive towards the dismantling of a stronghold of bitterness as you rebuild a stronghold of compassion in its place. However, God's grace comes in abundant supply so that you do not have to do it alone. *"And God is able to make all grace abound to you, that always having all sufficiency in everything, you may have an abundance for every good deed."* (2 Corinthians 9:8)

Forgiveness is necessary if you want to live in the fullness of life that God offers His children. To harbor bitterness cheats you of so many blessings that a life in Christ has to offer. If you are struggling in this area, I encourage you to go back through this guide, step by step, and dismantle the stronghold of bitterness. Rebuild in its place a stronghold of compassion by doing the activities that will starve bitterness and feed love for one another.

Lord Jesus, I am powerless to forgive. *My flesh wants vengeance, yet I know it is Your will that I forgive.* In the same manner that You have forgiven me of all my offenses, I choose right now to forgive my offender. I release _____ into your hands. I give up every "right" to harbor any resentment. I turn _____ completely over to You and declare Your blessing on his/her life. Give me the grace to renew my mind as I refuse to dwell on the feelings of unforgiveness as they resurface. Bring my emotions into alignment with my choice to forgive. Guide me as I strive to build a stronghold of compassion. Guard my heart so that no root of bitterness can spring up. Thank You for Your enabling Grace. Amen.